Look After Yourself

Your Hair

Look After Yourself

Your Hair

Claire Llewellyn

W
FRANKLIN WATTS
LONDON • SYDNEY

This edition 2004

Franklin Watts
96 Leonard Street
London
EC2A 4XD

Franklin Watts Australia
45-51 Huntley Street
Alexandria
NSW 2015

Copyright © Franklin Watts 2002

Series editor: Sarah Peutrill
Art director: Jonathan Hair
Design: Kirstie Billingham
Illustrations: James Evans
Photographs: Ray Moller unless otherwise acknowledged
Picture research: Diana Morris
Series consultant: Lynn Huggins-Cooper

Acknowledgments:
Dr Jeremy Burgess/Science Photo Library: 10cl
Eye of Science/Science Photo Library: 22b
Dr Chris Hale/Science Photo Library: 24bl
Manfred Kage/Science Photo Library: 10bl
David Scharf/Science Photo Library: 8
Superstock: 21b
Andrew Syred/Science Photo Library: 24tr

With thanks to our models: Alice, Emilia, Holly, Jerome, Lewis, Mandalena and Wilf

A CIP record for this book is available from the British Library.

Dewey Classification 613.2

ISBN: 0 7496 5646 8

Printed in Hong Kong/China

Contents

Looking at hair

There are many different sorts of hair. Your hair may be long or short or in-between. It may be curly, wavy or straight. It may be thick or fine. It may be red, black, brown, fair, grey or white.

What's your hair like?

Hair is one of the things that makes us look different from each other. But what is it, and what's it for?

Your hair has a particular colour and style. Do you know anyone with hair just like yours?

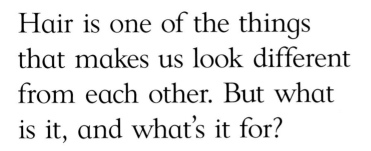

Your hair is one of the things that makes you look like YOU!

A head of hair

A hair is a silky, soft thread that grows out of the skin. It is made of a tough substance called keratin.

This picture has been magnified. It shows a hair growing out of the skin. The hair is made of tiny scales of keratin.

We have short, fine hairs all over our bodies. We have longer, thicker hair on our heads.

Most of us have about 100,000 hairs on our heads. About 50 drop out every day. New hairs take their place.

Hair protects your head from the Sun.

Hair helps to keep you warm in the cold.

Brr! You would soon feel chilly without your hair.

Your hair helps to keep you warm. It also protects your skin from the Sun's strong rays.

Messy hair

My hair seems to get messy all by itself!

Hair often gets messy. It gets in a mess when you sleep on it, fiddle with it or go out in the wind. The long hairs get tangled like spaghetti or bits of string!

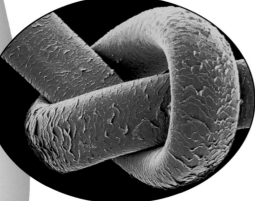

These hairs are magnified. The scales of keratin are lying flat and the hair is smooth.

Hair sometimes sticks up after a night's sleep.

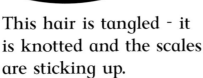

This hair is tangled - it is knotted and the scales are sticking up.

10

Brushing your hair keeps it tidy.
Brushing gets rid of tangles and
makes the hair lie flat.
Brushed hair looks
smooth and shiny.

Brush your
hair to keep
it tidy.

Brushing your
hair makes it
look better.

Brushes and combs

Keeping your hair tidy is easy. All you need is a brush and comb. A brush gets rid of old hairs and tiny specks of dirt. A comb makes a neat parting and keeps hair tidy.

How often do you brush your hair?

Hair is soft and breaks easily. Always brush it gently.

Brushes and combs soon get dirty. They need to be kept clean. Every two or three weeks, pull out old hairs from the bristles and teeth. Then wash your brush and comb in soapy water.

Hair gets dirty

Every hair on your head is coated with oil.
This protects it and keeps it healthy.
But specks of dirt stick to the oil and
make your hair dirty.

Dirty hair looks horrible!

Traffic makes the air dirty. The dirt then sticks to our hair.

When we are hot, our heads begin to sweat. Sweat is sticky and makes our hair smell. It needs to be washed away.

Running around makes us sweat. Our hair gets damp and sticky.

Washing also protects hair. The chlorine in swimming pools is very strong and can harm our hair. It's important to wash it away.

Always wash your hair after a swim.

Washing your hair

We all need to wash our hair once or twice a week. This helps to keep it clean.

Washing keeps your hair clean and shiny.

1 Wet the hair well.

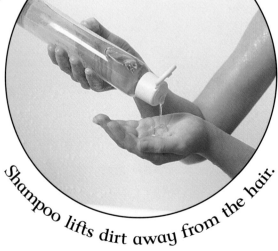

2 Pour some shampoo onto your hand and rub it into your hair.

Shampoo lifts dirt away from the hair.

3 Rub your hair gently near the roots. This is where it gets most dirty.

Water washes away the dirty bubbles.

4 Rinse off the bubbles with clean water.

5 Some people put conditioner on their hair. This protects it and makes it feel soft and look shiny.

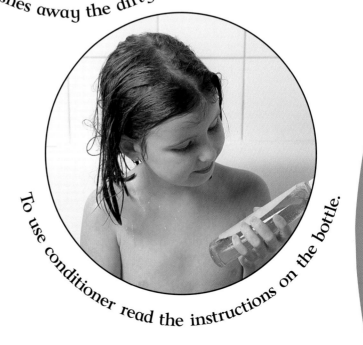

To use conditioner read the instructions on the bottle.

Drying your hair

After you have washed your hair, pat it gently with a towel. Try not to rub it or it will tangle. Wet hair breaks very easily, so comb it gently with a wide-toothed comb.

Don't rub your hair too hard. It will only break or tangle.

It's best for hair to dry on its own. Hairdryers are so hot they can scorch it. If you do use a hairdryer, always keep it moving and hold it away from your head.

Ouch! Hairdryers can burn your ears!

Thick hair takes a long time to dry. Fine hair dries more quickly.

Hairstyles

People wear their hair in all sorts of ways. Some people like short hair. Others prefer to grow it long and wear it in different styles.

I've got a trendy new haircut.

Long hair can be put in bunches.

Short hair is easy to look after.

Longer hair can be plaited.

Our hairstyle is one of the things that makes us look different.

People have different ideas about hairstyles. Would you wear your hair like this?

Having a haircut

Your hair never stops growing. It grows about 12 millimetres every month. As new hair grows from the root, the other end of the hair grows older and weaker. In time it may split.

I've got split ends — it's time for a haircut!

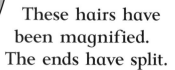

These hairs have been magnified. The ends have split.

To keep it healthy and strong, our hair needs to be cut about every two months. Cutting hair is skilled work. Never do it yourself!

Did you know that your hair grows more quickly in summer than winter?

This girl's hair is growing over her eyes.

After a haircut she can see better!

23

Head lice

Hair is thick and warm. Tiny creatures called head lice like to live in it. They lay their eggs (called nits) there.

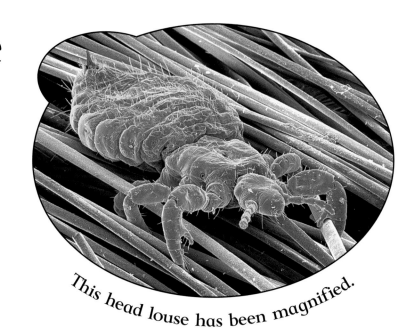

This head louse has been magnified.

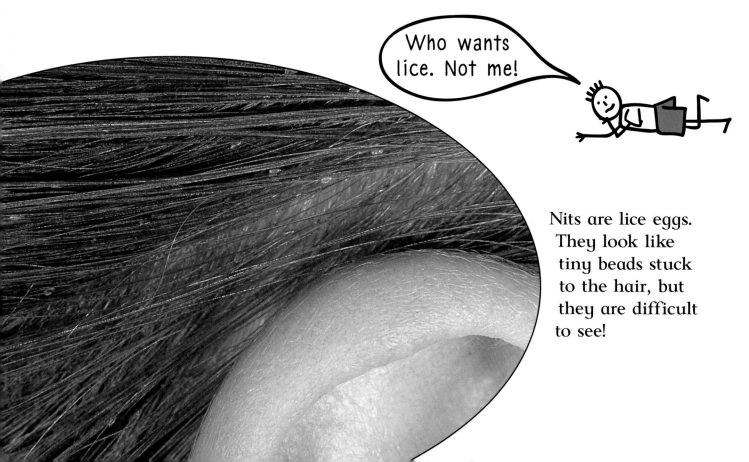

Who wants lice. Not me!

Nits are lice eggs. They look like tiny beads stuck to the hair, but they are difficult to see!

Most people get lice at some time or another. They spread quickly from head to head, and from brushes, combs and seat backs. Lice like clean hair because it's easier to move around in.

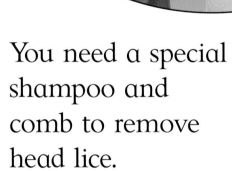

Getting head lice is unlucky. It doesn't mean your hair is dirty.

You need a special shampoo and comb to remove head lice.

Healthy hair

How can
I have shiny,
healthy-looking
hair?

Everyone wants healthy hair.
It looks so smooth and shiny.
Unhealthy hair looks dull
and flat.

These foods help to
make your hair strong.

The food you eat helps to make your
hair healthy. A good diet is important.
Some foods, like fish, chicken, cheese
and nuts, make your hair grow strong.

Other foods, such as fruit, vegetables, cereals and milk, help to keep it healthy.

These foods will help you have healthy hair.

Drinking lots of water is important for hair. It helps to keep hair shiny.

Water is very good for your hair.

Brush your hair every morning and wash it twice a week. That way, your hair will always look good!

27

Glossary

cereals   foods, such as those eaten at breakfast, that are made from wheat, oats, rice and other grasses

chlorine   a strong-smelling gas that is used to keep the water in swimming pools clean

conditioner   something that you put on your hair to make it soft and shiny

diet   the food that you usually eat

fair   having hair of a light colour

head lice   (singular: head louse) tiny insects that live in the hair

keratin   the material that hair is made of

magnified   made to look bigger

nit	the egg of a head louse
rinse	to wash away with water
root	the part of the hair that grows under the skin
scale	a tiny piece of keratin that overlaps others to make a hair
scorch	to burn slightly
shampoo	a liquid soap used for washing hair
style	the way you choose to have your hair
sweat	a salty, sticky liquid given off by the skin when you are hot
tangle	a small knot in the hair
thread	a very thin strand of something

Index

About this book

Learning the principles of how to keep healthy and clean is one of life's most important skills. **Look After Yourself** is a series aimed at young children who are just beginning to develop these skills. **Your Hair** looks at how to keep hair clean, tidy and healthy.

Here are a number of activities that children could try:

Pages 6-7 Collect photographs of people with different hair types.

Pages 8-9 Discuss how body hair helps to keep us warm - at cold temperatures hairs stand up, trapping warm air next to the skin. (As the hairs stand up we get goose pimples.)

Pages 10-11 Hold a section of hair near the root and run fingers carefully down the hair. Then do the same, but run the fingers up towards the root. With a little concentration, the hair feels smooth running down, but rough running up. This is because running fingers towards the root makes the scales stand up.

Pages 12-13 Ask children to design a comb or hairbrush that would be ideal for their own hair. Will the teeth or bristles be close or far apart, long or short? What kind of handle will it have?

Pages 14-15 Research the French pompadour - powdered styles that were fashionable before the French Revolution. The hair was so big and dirty then that mice nested inside!

Pages 16-17 Collect a range of shampoos and conditioners and look at the instructions for using them. Are they all the same? Ask children to design their own shampoo labels. What will their shampoo do? What will it be called?

Pages 18-19 Write step-by-step instructions for using a hairdryer.

Pages 20-21 Conduct a survey of the different hairstyles in a class or group. Which is the most popular way to keep hair - short or long? Which is the favourite way for long hair to be worn?

Pages 22-23 Interview a hairdresser about his or her job.

Pages 24-25 Study the life-cycle of a head louse.

Pages 26-27 Create some 'recipes for healthy hair' using the foods that are good for hair.